More Miniature
Oriental Rugs
& Carpets

Madonna and Child with Canon van der Paele, 1434 (oil on panel)
by Jan van Eyck (*c*.1390–1441)

More Miniature Oriental Rugs & Carpets

Meik and Ian McNaughton

GUILD OF MASTER CRAFTSMAN PUBLICATIONS LTD

First published 2000 by
Guild of Master Craftsman Publications Ltd
Castle Place, 166 High Street,
Lewes, East Sussex BN7 1XU

Photographs by Peter Wright
Stitching charts produced by Peter Rhodes
Line drawings by John Yates

ISBN 1 86108 154 5

A catalogue record for this book is available from the British Library.

Edited by Stephen Haynes
Cover and book design by Wheelhouse Design, Brighton

Set in Cygnet and Cheltenham

Colour origination by Viscan Graphics, Singapore
Printed and bound by Kyodo Printing, Singapore

Measurements

Although care has been taken to ensure that imperial measurements are true and accurate, they are only conversions from metric and have been rounded up or down to the nearest ⅛in. Care should therefore be taken to use either imperial or metric measurements consistently. The exact size of the finished designs is dependent on the stitch count and the gauge of canvas used.

Contents

Turkey

The Caucasus

Iran

Central Asia

Introduction

My wife and I were much encouraged by the reception accorded to our first book on making miniature oriental rugs and carpets, and we now offer dolls' house and miniatures enthusiasts a further collection of designs based on the conventional scale of one-twelfth full size. A carpet for a dolls' house need not be larger than about 200 x 125mm (8 x 5in), and in many cases 150 x 100mm (6 x 4 in) would be big enough. With this scale in mind, we needed only to look at rugs under 2.5m (8ft) in length and to choose designs which could be miniaturized without losing the essential features and character of the original.

Even when narrowing the field of choice to this extent, there was still the problem of fitting the maximum amount of detail into a small area. This meant using the highest stitch count with which it was practical to work. Using crewel wool, with which my wife preferred to work, the most satisfactory solution was to use 24-count canvas.

The next important step was to produce a charted pattern that was clear and easy to follow. This meant that it had to be in colour and at a larger scale than the finished carpet. The original charts were made on graph paper ruled in inches and tenths, and the more heavily ruled inch lines were invaluable guides when following the pattern. The charts in this book are already at a larger scale than the finished carpets, but users need not hesitate to have them further enlarged if they have any difficulty in following them.

The present collection consists of 24 designs, with a wide geographical spread covering all the principal weaving areas. Four of the designs are based on rugs in our own collection and a further six on rugs owned by other members of our family. One is based on the painting by Jan van Eyck reproduced as the frontispiece. The remaining thirteen are based on rugs included in illustrated sale catalogues produced by the principal auction houses; a list is included at page 93.

For the purposes of this book, the designs are grouped in four sections, covering Turkey, the Caucasus, Iran and central Asia. We have tried to include both antique and more modern examples to widen the choice on offer. In this way, the similarities in design within each region can be appreciated and the contrasts between one and another underlined.

This book is primarily intended to provide dolls' house enthusiasts with a range of rug and carpet designs to suit most furnishing schemes. We hope it will also appeal to those who do needlework for its own sake, who may find stitching these miniature carpets a satisfying occupation. Each design is presented with a full-size picture of the finished piece, a little information about its background and a clear colour chart from which to work.

Ian McNaughton

Materials and Techniques

Materials

Canvas

All the carpets in this book should be worked on 24-count canvas. Included in the information for each design is a precise stitch count and an approximate finished size for the piece. When cutting the canvas for a particular carpet, allow about 75mm (3in) extra at each end and 50mm (2in) on each side. This will make it much easier to block or stretch the finished work.

With a very fine-pointed pencil (never a ball-point pen, as this can show through the paler threads), mark the central lines on the canvas (indicated by small arrows on each chart) and then the heavier lines shown on the chart. These should come every 10 holes, and will serve as helpful guidelines when counting stitches and following the pattern. Using such guidelines will also mean that you can spot mistakes at an early stage, so unpicking should not be so depressing as it might otherwise be. It is important, therefore, to check carefully that the marking out is correct before proceeding further.

Frames

There are several types of small frame available, but the choice of which to use is a very personal thing. It is, of course, possible to work without a frame if you prefer, but this does make straightening the finished work much more difficult. If you are using a frame to keep the canvas taut, you will find it necessary to make each individual stitch in two separate movements, with a hand on either side of the frame. This may seem cumbersome to begin with, but it quickly becomes much easier.

Threads

The thread recommended for working these rugs is Appletons crewel wool. A single strand will suffice. This wool is very fine and soft, so do not use threads longer than 30–35cm (12–14in), as they tend to pull apart with wear. If the wool looks very thin at any point, it is best to cut that part out before starting to stitch, but sometimes the thin parts only appear after work has begun. When this happens, the easiest thing is to work two stitches on top of one another.

Alternatively, two threads of stranded cotton (Anchor or DMC) can be used. Stranded cotton is easier to work with than crewel wool, but does not give such a warm and realistic finish. It is also harder to block and stretch than wool.

The suggested shade numbers given for each rug apply to Appletons crewel wool, but a table of equivalent shade numbers for Anchor and DMC cottons can be found on pages 94–6. Note that the colours used on the charts have been chosen for clarity and contrast, and do not necessarily match accurately the colours of the rugs themselves.

Needles

Use a size 24 tapestry needle with a single strand of Appletons crewel wool, or a size 26 needle with two threads of Anchor or DMC stranded cotton. As with frames, however, the size of needle is really a matter of personal choice: some people like working with small needles, others do not.

Techniques

Tent stitch

All the carpets are worked in tent stitch (see the diagrams below), which gives the neatest and flattest finish. Try to keep the back of the carpet as tidy as possible and looking almost the same as the front, by working the casting-on and -off thread ends underneath the stitching on the back. If the back is kept neat, there should be no need for any backing fabric to be used.

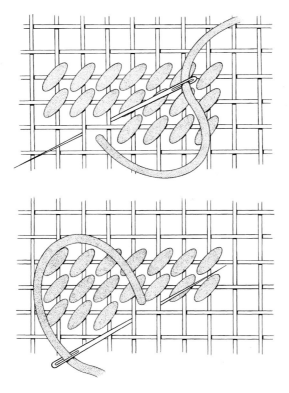

Tent stitch

Where to start stitching

The best place to start stitching seems to be a matter for debate. Some recommend beginning in the middle of the design, but it seems more logical to start on the centre line at one end of the carpet. Make sure that you have got the position of this central line exactly right as indicated on the chart, then work the border first, using just one colour for a while. Everyone has their own preferred method of working, however, and it is difficult to lay down any hard and fast rules.

Mistakes

If you make a mistake and discover your error before you have worked too many more stitches, simply unpick back to the incorrect part and put it right. As long as you check back frequently against the chart and the gridlines marked on the canvas, a mistake should never be too serious. Once the work is finished, if you discover that one stitch is in the wrong colour, it is often possible to cover this with a stitch of the right colour. If a small mistake on your oriental rug cannot be rectified, just remember the old saying: 'Only Allah is perfect.'

Blocking

When the stitching is finished, remove the canvas from the frame and block it to straighten the carpet. Dampen the canvas and stretch it out on a board with drawing pins, taking care to ensure that the corners are square and the sides parallel. Leave it on the board until the threads are quite dry.

Finishing the long side edges

To finish off the long side edges of the carpet, cut the excess canvas back to two threads and then work a plaited edging stitch into the last row of stitching, following the steps given below and starting at the top right-hand corner with the cut edge of the canvas uppermost (see the diagrams opposite).

1 Bring the needle from the back of the canvas to the front, leaving 50mm (2in) of wool lying along the top edge (where it can be held by your free hand). This will be covered by subsequent stitches.
2 Take the needle through the next hole to the left, again from back to front.

3 Now take the needle back to the original hole again, thus forming an 'x' stitch over the top of the canvas.
4 Carry the needle forward three holes (i.e. missing out two holes) and bring it through the canvas from back to front.
5 Then take the needle back two holes (i.e. missing out one) and bring it through the canvas from back to front once more.

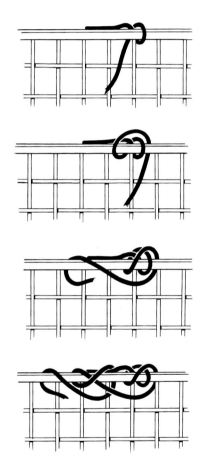

Plaited edging stitch for the long sides

Continue the plait, taking the needle three holes on and two holes back as set out above, always remembering that the needle should pass through the canvas from back to front.

Materials and
Techniques

Fringing the ends

The fringes at either end of the rug should be worked in a Turkey or Ghiordes knot. Using a double thread, take this through the canvas as shown in the diagram below and pull the knot fairly tight. The knots should be worked through the row of holes immediately after the last row of stitching. Leave a loop of about 20mm (¾in) before moving on to the next hole. The wool can be passed round a pencil to form even loops, but the end of a finger is just as good and much simpler.

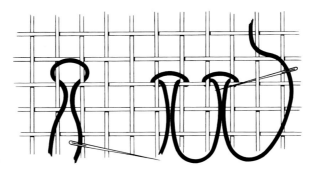

Turkey or Ghiordes knot for the fringes on the short ends of the rug

When the knotting is complete, cut the loops and trim the ends to form a neat fringe. Finally, trim the excess canvas back to three threads and use a little Copydex or other adhesive to fix the underside of the fringe to it.

Designing your own carpets

After studying this book and following the charts to stitch some of the carpets featured here, you may feel that you would like to make a miniature version of your own favourite fireside rug. The following points will help you to produce a workable design.

1 The rug you select for miniaturization should have a rectilinear pattern, free from curved lines, and the general layout should be bold, without fussy detail. This will enable

the design to be adapted to the smaller scale without too much character being lost.

2 Establish the approximate size of the proposed miniature at 1/12 scale and with 24 stitches to the inch (to match the 24-count canvas). If, for example, your original rug measures 183 x 122cm (6 x 4ft), the 1/12 scale miniature at 15 x 10cm (6 x 4in) will be about 144 x 96 stitches. The exact size will emerge later.

3 Look at the proportions of your rug and, in particular, the relative widths of the field and borders. Commonly the field width is about three-fifths of the total width. In the example mentioned above, therefore, the field would be about 57 stitches wide, with each border 19 stitches wide, but you will need to work out the proportions to suit your own rug.

4 Study the main border of your rug and sketch its principal repeating motif, reducing the size of the design as far as possible without losing the basic idea behind it. Work out how many times this repeat will fit into the available length and width of the miniature, allowing for the narrow subsidiary borders or 'guards'.

5 With the borders fixed, you can establish the final overall size of the rug; the size of the field will also become clear in the process. Remember that normally the field must have an odd number of stitches in both length and width, because of the centre lines. You may also need to make small adjustments to the length and width to ensure that the corner patterns fit neatly; this is often the hardest part.

6 Draw out the field on squared paper and mark the centre lines. Fit the main field motifs into the space available by reducing their sizes in proportion to the miniature. In the case of small repeated motifs, the total number can be reduced in order to improve clarity.

7 Draw out the complete chart for the rug, including borders, and colour in the squares appropriately.

Materials and
Techniques

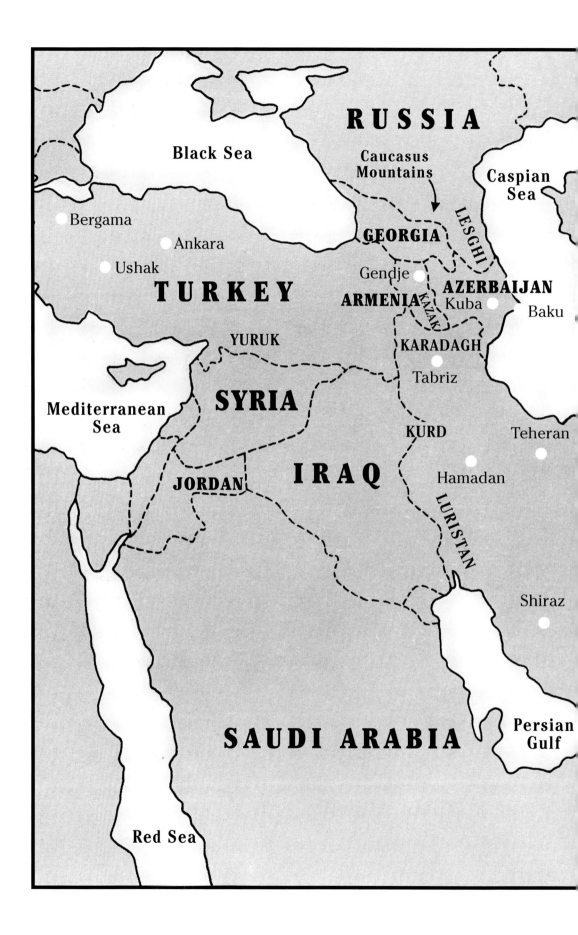

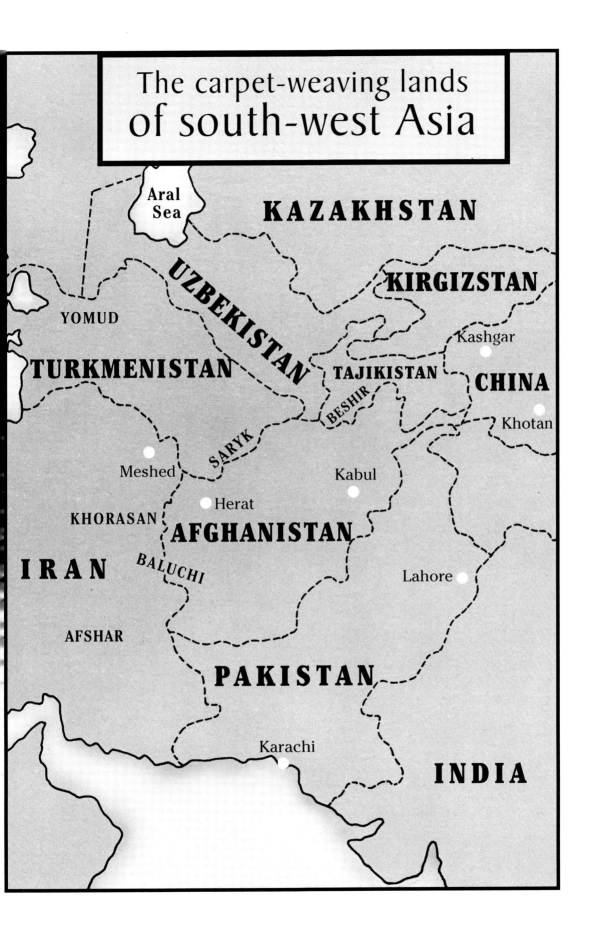

The carpet-weaving lands of south-west Asia

TURKEY

Introduction

 Although carpets woven in Anatolia (Asian Turkey) have been coming to Western Europe for more than 500 years, few have survived to the present day and our knowledge of them derives principally from the number that appear in religious paintings of the period, chiefly in works by Italian and Flemish artists. In several examples a carpet is depicted under the throne of the Virgin Mary with a latticed pattern of stars and crosses which itself was based on the tessellated floor of a church in Anatolia. The first carpet in the present collection is of this genre; it is based on a carpet appearing in a painting by Jan van Eyck, dating from 1434.

Many Turkish weavings take the form of a prayer rug, with arch or mihrab (prayer niche) at one end, but those from the village of Ladik in central Anatolia are unusual in that the arch is in the middle of the rug, below a row of tulip-like flowers. An example is no. 2 in this collection.

Carpet weaving continues in Turkey as a cottage industry, in villages with a centuries-old tradition; it is officially encouraged and natural vegetable dyes have been reintroduced. An example of a rug produced under this scheme is our no. 4.

1

Geometric design after Jan van Eyck

FIFTEENTH CENTURY

Size (excluding fringes): 153 x 111mm (6 x 4⅜in)
Stitch count: 145 x 103

This design is based on a carpet appearing in a painting by the Flemish artist Jan van Eyck known as *Madonna and Child with Canon van der Paele*, a reproduction of which is included as a frontispiece to this book. The field design of the original was probably based on the mosaic-tiled floor of a church.

	209			358
	206			644
	926			843
	921			988 and fringes

15

TURKEY
Geometric
design after
Jan van Eyck

2
Ladik prayer rug

NINETEENTH CENTURY

Size (excluding fringes): 142 x 110 mm (5½ x 4⅜in)

Stitch count: 135 x 95

Ladik lies in central Anatolia to the north of Konya, and was famous for its prayer rugs from the eighteenth to the early twentieth century. The tulip-like flowers above the prayer arch are characteristic of Ladik weaving.

███	504	▓▓▓	116
███	748	☐	991
░░░	525	☐	988 and fringes
░░░	692		

More Miniature
Oriental Rugs
and Carpets

4

Modern
Turkish rug

TWENTIETH CENTURY

Size (excluding fringes): 162 x 112mm (6⅜ x 4⅜in)

Stitch count: 155 x 101

From its colouring, and in particular the dark blue field, it might be thought that this rug had Baluchi origins; however, it was woven in the Anatolian village of Yagcibedir under a government-supported scheme to encourage a recovery in carpet weaving by forming village co-operatives.

224		185	
227		992 and fringes	
749			

More Miniature
Oriental Rugs
and Carpets

THE
CAUCASUS

Introduction

 The Caucasus Mountains, stretching from the Black Sea to the Caspian Sea, and the surrounding area are home to a number of distinct ethnic groups with their own languages, religions and characters. Carpet weaving has been carried on in the region for many centuries and, though each weaving area has its own distinctive patterns and motifs, common characteristics include the use of bold primary colours and straight lines rather than curves to outline the various features of the pattern. Caucasian rugs are generally fairly small, seldom exceeding two metres (6ft 6in) in length; this makes them very suitable for miniaturization.

The best of Caucasian weaving dates from the nineteenth century, at the start of which the area was under Persian domination, and many of the designs and motifs used are derived from earlier Persian weaving, though they have become distorted as time has passed. During the twentieth century, under Soviet influence, much of the weaving was concentrated in workshops and collectives and the earlier free designs became more stilted and less attractive.

Amongst the principal weaving areas was Kazak, on the southern slope of the Caucasus in the state of Azerbaijan; bright colours and bold patterns make Kazak rugs easy to recognize. Three are included in this section. In neighbouring Armenia, with its long Christian traditions, the use of various cross motifs is characteristic; one example is included.

On the eastern slopes of the Caucasus, along the shores of the Caspian Sea, several weaving areas produce rugs with repeated stars or geometrical shapes (*guls*) in bright colours. Examples from Kuba and Moghan are included.

5

Kuba runner

LATE NINETEENTH CENTURY

Size (excluding fringes): 166 x 83mm (6½ x 3¼in)

Stitch count: 162 x 75 (extensible by increments of 36)

Kuba lies on the eastern slope of the Caucasus, not far from the Caspian Sea. The area was well known for its long rugs or 'runners', and this colourful example has been specially designed so that it can be lengthened as required for passages or hallways. Care should be taken to maintain the colour sequences of the field motifs.

■	226		992 and fringes
▨	184		922
□	842	■	926
▨	644		

29

THE
CAUCASUS
Kuba runner

6

Moghan rug

c. 1900

Size (excluding fringes): 150 x 113mm (6 x 4½in)
Stitch count: 144 x 101

The Moghan steppes in the south of Azerbaijan were home to several nomadic tribes, particularly before the border between Russia and Persia became finally established. This small rug displays a field charged with a double row of polychrome 'Memling *guls*', as described in the introduction to carpet no. 3 (see page 20).

■	504	▨	692	
■	852	☐	992	
▨	853	▨	988 fringes	
▨	156			

More Miniature
Oriental Rugs
and Carpets

7

Daghestan prayer rug

LATE NINETEENTH CENTURY

Size (excluding fringes): 194 x 104mm (7¾ x 4in)

Stitch count: 183 x 95

This design of prayer rug is typical of the eastern part of the Caucasus region. The arch is always angular and the latticed field is usually filled with flowers, as in the present case; the colours are soft and harmonious.

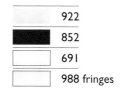

■	504	░	922
■	721	■	852
□	842	□	691
░	762	□	988 fringes
░	404		

35

THE
CAUCASUS
Daghestan
prayer rug

8

Armenian
stepped-cross rug

LATE NINETEENTH CENTURY

Size (excluding fringes): 190 x 115 mm (7½ x 4½in)
Stitch count: 172 x 100

This pleasing rug, whose simple stepped-cross pattern confirms its Christian origins, may not have been woven within the boundaries of present-day Armenia, since in the nineteenth century Armenian communities were widespread throughout the region. When stitching this rug, note the use of lines to superimpose crosses on the field motifs overall.

▨	721	▨	693
▨	724	▨	696
▨	923	✚	915
▨	925	▢	988 and fringes
▨	929		

More Miniature
Oriental Rugs
and Carpets

9

'Star' Kazak rug

NINETEENTH CENTURY

Size (excluding fringes): 170 x 118 mm (6¾ x 4⅝in)
Stitch count: 165 x 107

'Star' Kazaks, with their bold pattern and varied colouring, are rare and eagerly sought after. The origin of the design is obscure, but the central stars seem to be guarded by four green dragons with rudimentary red feet.

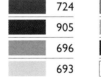

724	644
905	742
696	747
693	988 and fringes

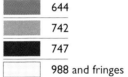

41

THE
CAUCASUS
'Star' Kazak rug

10

Sewan Kazak rug

EARLY TWENTIETH CENTURY

Size (excluding fringes): 175 x 108mm (7 x 4¼in)

Stitch count: 165 x 101

This design, with the centre field displaying bold latch-hook devices, is another classic Kazak style in typical strong colours.

▬	504	░	692
■	852	☐	988 and fringes
▬	293		

44

11

Chondzoresk Kazak rug

*c.*1900

Size (excluding fringes): 163 x 117 mm (6½ x 4⅝in)
Stitch count: 155 x 105

Sometimes described as 'cloud-band' Kazaks, these rugs have a field containing two or three large medallions in different colours. At the centre of each medallion there is a very curious swastika-like device in a yellow rectangle.

47

THE
CAUCASUS
Chondzoresk
Kazak rug

12

South Caucasian animal rug

LATE NINETEENTH CENTURY

Size (excluding fringes): 178 x 114 mm (7 x 4½in)
Stitch count: 173 x 103

This colourful rug, with its polychrome bands containing quadrupeds, trees and other devices, is attractively different from most Caucasian weavings.

■	207	□	842	
■	926	▨	912	
■	295	□	988 and fringes	

More Miniature
Oriental Rugs
and Carpets

13

Talish long rug

LATE NINETEENTH CENTURY

Size (excluding fringes): 155 x 92mm (6⅛ x 3⅝in)
Stitch count: 147 x 87

Talish rugs come from the southern border area of Azerbaijan, on the shores of the Caspian Sea. They are usually long and narrow, with the field of plain dark blue or sea-green only one-third the width of the rug. The design has been arranged so that a longer version can be stitched if required by adding an extra 40 stitches to the length, without upsetting the border sequence.

More Miniature
Oriental Rugs
and Carpets

■	226	▨	694
■	749	□	992 and fringes
■	157		

THE
CAUCASUS
Talish long rug

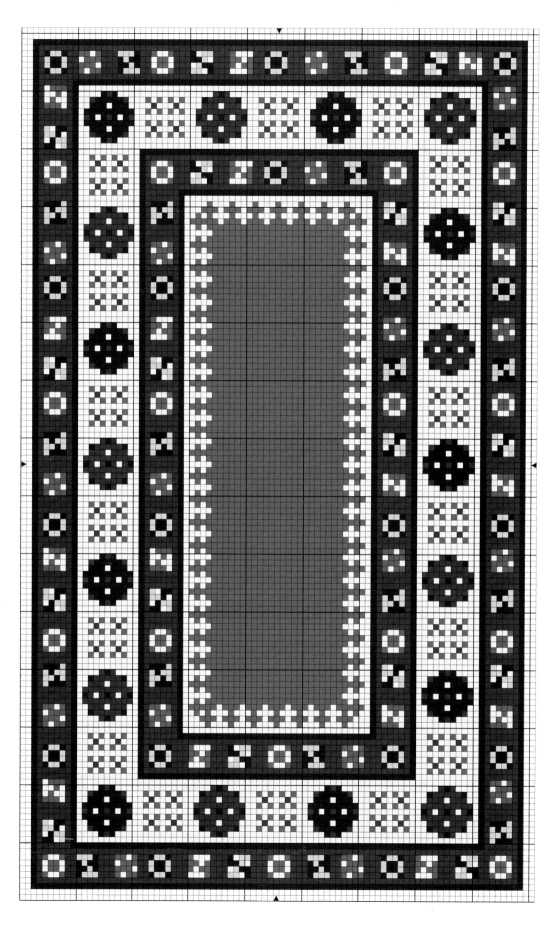

IRAN

Introduction

Because their complex designs cannot be scaled down convincingly, this book does not include any examples from the famous carpet workshops of central Iran; nevertheless, there are a number of provincial centres and tribal areas which produce material very suitable for miniaturization.

In the north-west of Iran, near the frontier with Turkey, there are nomadic Kurdish tribes with a weaving tradition in respect of both pile rugs and flat-woven kilims; an example of the former is included.

Further to the south lies the city of Hamadan, the centre of a large weaving area which produces a wide variety of designs and styles. Three examples attributed to the Hamadan area are included in this section (nos. 15–17); they are based on small rugs that were in my mother's possession from her early youth. Similar in size, weave and colouring, they clearly have a common origin and, because they are small – less than a metre (39in) in length – it has been possible to reproduce their designs in considerable detail, in some areas stitch for stitch. The resulting miniatures have an unusual delicacy.

In the southern province of Kerman, the Afshar tribe produce rugs with geometric features similar to those found in Caucasian weaving; this is explained by the tribe's Turkoman origin. They were settled originally in Azerbaijan, but forced to move to their present area in the sixteenth century. One example of Afshar work is included here as no. 18.

In the north-eastern province of Khorasan, along the border with Afghanistan, live various Baluchi tribes, some settled in villages and some still nomadic. They produce a variety of rugs and carpets in a characteristic range of colours, including reds, browns and dark blue, with the field background often in a natural camel-hair shade. Their patterns and motifs have been influenced by both Persian and Turkoman weavings. Three examples are included in this section.

14

Kurdish rug

EARLY TWENTIETH CENTURY

Size (excluding fringes): 169 x 111mm (6¾ x 4⅜in)
Stitch count: 161 x 105

The field pattern of this rug is of a repetitive design which has been used for rugs and also for all kinds of bag faces and other containers. The muted colours are typical of Kurdish weaving.

■	326	■	759
■	324	■	207
■	322	■	184
■	293	□	988 and fringes

59

IRAN
Kurdish rug

15

'Crab' rug

c.1900

Size (excluding fringes): 175 x 103mm (7 x 4in)
Stitch count: 165 x 95

Having no formal provenance for this and the two succeeding rugs, it was necessary to give them names for identification purposes. It was no problem for this rug, as the two fearsome creatures in the field will confirm.

■	225	■	187	
■	749	☐	691	
▨	155	☐	988	fringes

More Miniature
Oriental Rugs
and Carpets

16

'Star' rug

*c.*1900

Size (excluding fringes): 180 x 110mm (7 x 4¼in)

Stitch count: 171 x 103

This attractive and colourful rug was also easy to name, with the multiple octagons in the field each containing an eight-pointed star.

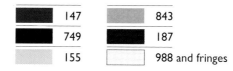

■	147	▨	843	
■	749	■	187	
▨	155	□	988 and fringes	

65

IRAN
'Star' rug

17

'Hook'
medallion rug

*c.*1900

Size (excluding fringes): 168 x 111mm (6⅝ x 4⅜in)
Stitch count: 161 x 105

The small size of the original made it possible to reproduce this
wonderful centre medallion in realistic detail, together with the
elaborate multicoloured floral border.

▮ 147		▮ 184	
▮ 749		▮ 585	
▮ 923		☐ 761 and fringes	

More Miniature
Oriental Rugs
and Carpets

18

Afshar rug

LATE NINETEENTH CENTURY
Size (excluding fringes): 143 x 115mm (5¾ x 4½in)
Stitch count: 135 x 105

Originally nomadic, the majority of the Afshar tribe are now settled. Their rugs have a wide variety of patterns, some relating to their Turkoman origins and others influenced by the customs and traditions of the area in which they now live. The latter account for the comma-like *botehs* on each side of the light blue field of this rug. In the nineteenth century the city of Kerman was famous for its shawls, on which the principal motif was the *boteh*.

■	504		□	842
■	852		□	992
▨	743		□	988 fringes
▨	912			

71

IRAN
Afshar rug

19

Baluchi
palmette rug

TWENTIETH CENTURY

Size (excluding fringes): 166 x 110mm (6½ x 4¼in)

Stitch count: 161 x 99

The repeated devices filling the field of this rug are sometimes described as 'tarantulas', and they occur in some Caucasian carpets. In the present case they were probably used by the Baluchi weaver because they made a satisfying pattern; they are attractively set off by the white scrolled S-border.

■	227	▨	762
■	748	▨	882
■	185	☐	761 fringes
■	696		

More Miniature
Oriental Rugs
and Carpets

20

Baluchi
bag-face rug

*c.*1900

Size (excluding fringes): 175 x 110 mm (7 x 4¼in)

Stitch count: 167 x 103

A century ago, when most Baluchi tribes were still living a nomadic life, they produced a wide range of functional items, often based on designs from other areas. This rug design has been derived from a Baluchi saddle-bag face in the authors' collection; it displays a degree of Turkoman influence.

▰	749	▰	762
▰	726	▰	925
▰	721	▱	988 and fringes
▰	583		

More Miniature
Oriental Rugs
and Carpets

IRAN
Baluchi
bag-face rug

21

Baluchi stepped-cross carpet

NINETEENTH CENTURY

Size (excluding fringes): 172 x 98 mm (6¾ x 4in)

Stitch count: 161 x 91

This carpet, although woven in typical colouring, displays some features that suggest a Caucasian influence: in particular the archaic stepped crosses themselves and their diagonal arrangement by colour.

■	209	▨	762
■	925	☐	992
■	187	☐	988 fringes

More Miniature
Oriental Rugs
and Carpets

CENTRAL ASIA

Introduction

This region – which, for the purposes of this book, includes the areas of East and West Turkestan, stretching from the Chinese province of Sinkiang to the eastern shores of the Caspian Sea – was home to two very different traditions of carpet weaving. In the east, along the route of the 'Silk Road', the old overland trade route between China and the Middle East, carpets of high quality were woven in the oasis cities of Khotan, Yarkand and Kashgar in Sinkiang. In contrast, West Turkestan was largely populated by nomadic tribes who relied upon their weaving skills to provide themselves with a wide range of items for their own domestic use. These included bags and containers of many kinds, tent floors and door screens, camel and horse trappings and large pannier bags for use on their migrations. Much of the weaving was functional rather than decorative, but some very fine items were woven for special occasions such as weddings. As nomadic tribes became settled, they turned to making carpets and rugs for sale, gradually adjusting their sizes and shapes to meet the requirements of the market.

Though each tribe had its own traditional patterns and motifs, the weavings of the area display characteristic similarities in style and layout. The background colour is usually a dull red, with the field filled with repeated shapes known as *guls*: these may be large or small, simple or complex in design, but are almost always octagons or lozenges. The borders are normally filled with a repeating pattern in black or very dark blue, although some nineteenth-century carpets include brighter colours. Two rather unusual examples of tribal weaving have been included in this section, together with one carpet from Khotan.

Tribal weaving throughout the region has been badly affected by wars and political upheavals, and thus far fewer genuine carpets are being woven at the present time. In their place a modern carpet industry has emerged in nearby Pakistan, where many of the traditional Afghan and Turkoman designs are being made under workshop conditions.

22

Saryk Ak-Su rug

LATE NINETEENTH CENTURY

Size (excluding fringes): 191 x 117 mm (7½ x 4⅝in)

Stitch count: 185 x 105

The Saryk tribe, like most of the nomadic tribes of West Turkestan, used an octagonal *gul* on a dull red field for their principal weavings, but for some purposes used the pattern known as 'Ak-Su', as for the field of this rug. It is unusual and attractively different.

▮	852	▮	184
▮	148	▮	585
▮	207	▯	691 and fringes

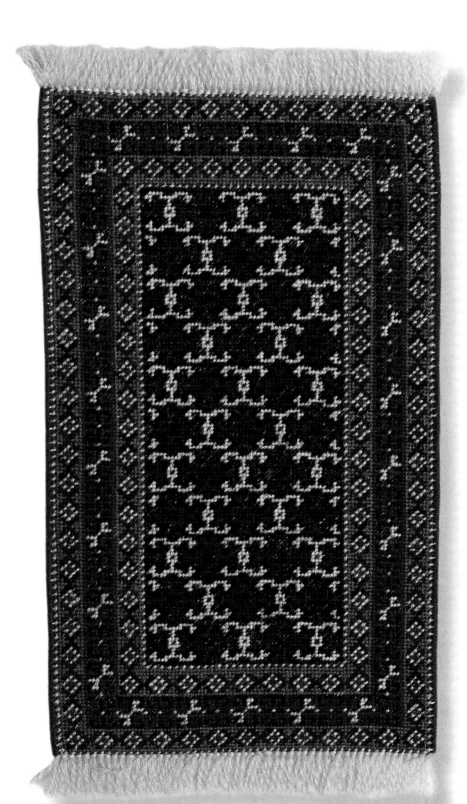

85

CENTRAL ASIA
Saryk Ak-Su rug

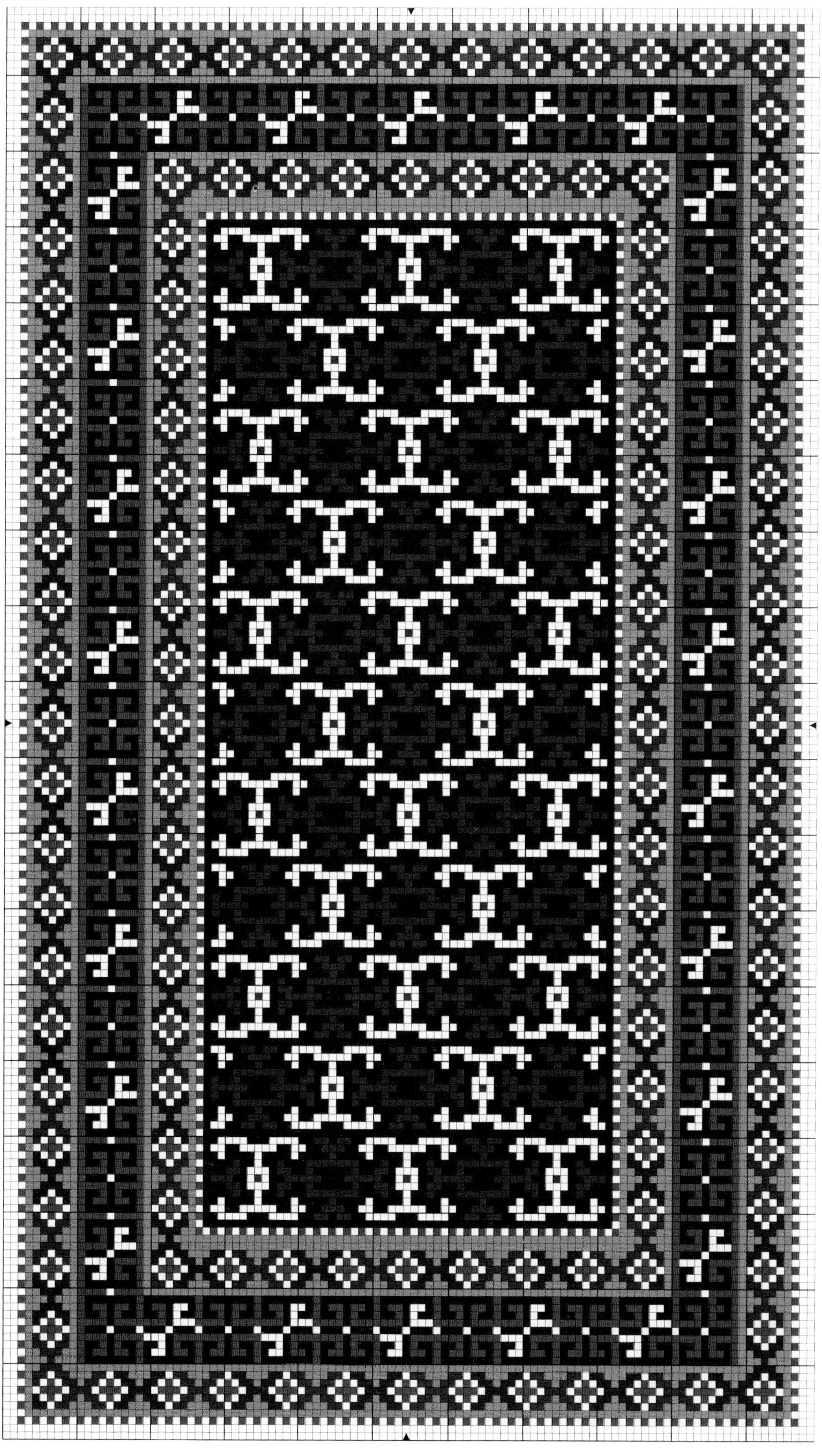

23

Yomud rug

LATE NINETEENTH CENTURY

Size (excluding fringes): 174 x 116 mm (6⅞ x 4½in)

Stitch count: 169 x 105

The Yomud tribes, who roamed the steppes to the east of the Caspian Sea, used a variety of *guls*, but all were lozenge-shaped and arranged in a diagonal pattern. In the present rug, the *guls* are arranged as if threaded on vertical barber's poles, against an unusually coloured background of pale blue, red-brown and purple.

▬	724	▬	565
▬	934	□	988 and fringes

More Miniature
Oriental Rugs
and Carpets

24

Khotan carpet

MID-NINETEENTH CENTURY

Size (excluding fringes): 156 x 105 mm (6⅛ x 4⅛in)

Stitch count: 147 x 99

Carpets with various versions of this design, with pomegranate trees growing from terracotta pots on a blue field, symbolic of life and plenty, were woven in both Khotan and Yarkand during the nineteenth century. Some had the field crowded with as many as four separate trees, with pots at each end of the field, but in order to ease miniaturization the present design contains only a single tree. The outer border consists of a series of linked swastikas, a symbol of happiness.

721	692
324	184
641	988 fringes

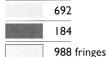

91

CENTRAL ASIA
Khotan carpet

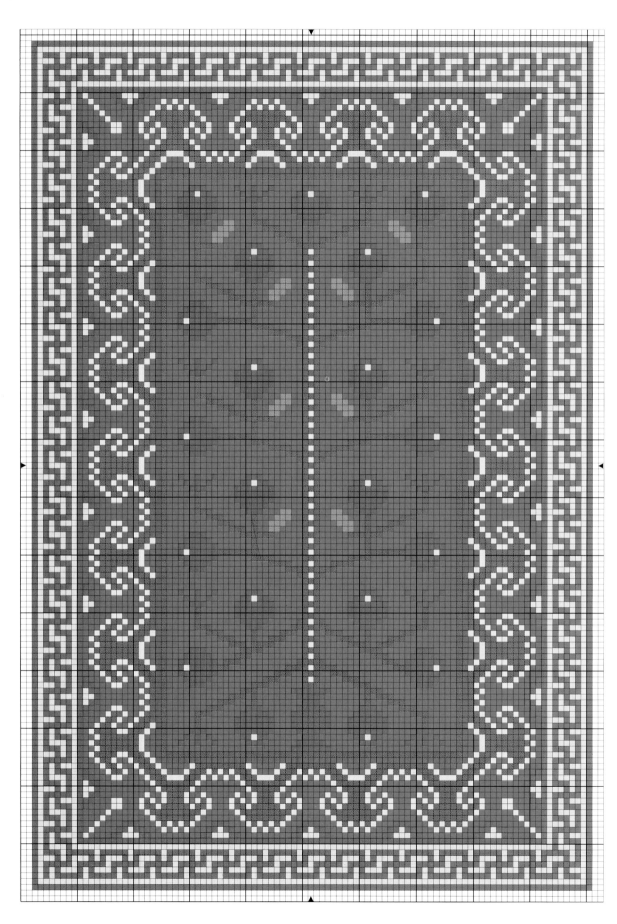

Sources

Thanks are due to the Groeningemuseum, Bruges, Belgium and the Bridgeman Art Library for permission to reproduce the painting by Jan van Eyck used for the frontispiece, on which the rug design no. 1 is modelled. The remaining designs have been freely adapted by the authors from the following sources:

Authors' collection: nos. 4, 14, 19, 20

Authors' family: nos. 8, 15, 16, 17, 21, 23

Christie's catalogues: nos. 2, 5, 6, 12, 13, 18, 22, 24

Renz GmbH, Frankfurt/Main: no. 10

Sotheby's catalogues: nos. 3, 7, 9, 11

Equivalent
shade numbers

For Appletons crewel wool and DMC and Anchor
stranded cottons

APPLETONS	DMC	ANCHOR
	Reds and pinks	
147	815	43
148	814	45
207	356	5975
209	355	5968
224	3328	39
225	347	1025
226	498	1005
227	221	896
504	321	19
721	356	5975
724	3830	1014
726	355	1014
759	3685	70
948	326	59

Browns

116	420	374
184	841	378
185	840	379
187	838	381
206	3778	1013
583	938	381
585	3371	382
696	782	308
724	3830	5975
762	738	361
905	433	371
912	436	374
915	869	944

White/ecru

691	543	933
761	739	366
882	746	275
988	762	234
991	Blanc neige	2
992	712 or ecru	387 or 926

Yellows

474	3827	1001
475	977	1002
692	739	366
693	729	887
694	3821	297
841	746	275
842	677	300
843	676	891

95

Equivalent
shade numbers

Greens

156	3768	779
157	924	851
293	522	860
295	305	268
358	3362	263
404	469	267
525	503	875
641	927	876
644	926	878

Blues

155	3809	1066
322	931	1034
324	920 ? 930	1035
326	3750	1036
565	517	162
742	794	176
743	341	120
747	336	150
748	336	150
749	823	127
852	823	127
853	341	120
921	318	235
922	932	920
923	931	1034
925	312	1036
926	311	1035
929	336	150
934	550	101

Black

993	310	403

About the Authors

Meik and Ian McNaughton, now retired, have lived in the Hampshire village of Chawton since 1963. Ian met Meik, who was born and grew up in Holland, while he was serving with the Royal Engineers in that country in the summer of 1945. They were married in the following year. Army life took them and their two daughters to Cyprus from 1955 to 1958 and to Germany from 1960 to 1963, when Ian retired from the army as a lieutenant-colonel to join the Railway Inspectorate of the Ministry of Transport. He finally retired from the position of Chief Inspecting Officer of Railways in 1982.

Ian has had a lifelong interest in oriental carpets. Meik has been sewing since her school days, when she learnt dressmaking and smocking. She started doing tapestry in the late 1950s and then took up counted cross stitch and patchwork in the late 1970s. Miniature oriental carpets appeared on the scene more recently, when a granddaughter reached dolls' house age.

Index

More Miniature
Oriental Rugs
and Carpets

TITLES AVAILABLE FROM
GMC Publications

BOOKS

DOLLS' HOUSES AND MINIATURES

Architecture for Dolls' Houses	*Joyce Percival*
A Beginners' Guide to the Dolls' House Hobby	*Jean Nisbett*
The Complete Dolls' House Book	*Jean Nisbett*
The Dolls' House 1/24 Scale: A Complete Introduction	*Jean Nisbett*
Dolls' House Accessories, Fixtures and Fittings	*Andrea Barham*
Dolls' House Bathrooms: Lots of Little Loos	*Patricia King*
Dolls' House Fireplaces and Stoves	*Patricia King*
Easy to Make Dolls' House Accessories	*Andrea Barham*
Heraldic Miniature Knights	*Peter Greenhill*
Make Your Own Dolls' House Furniture	*Maurice Harper*
Making Dolls' House Furniture	*Patricia King*
Making Georgian Dolls' Houses	*Derek Rowbottom*
Making Miniature Gardens	*Freida Gray*
Making Miniature Oriental Rugs & Carpets	*Meik & Ian McNaughton*
Making Period Dolls' House Accessories	*Andrea Barham*
Making 1/12 Scale Character Figures	*James Carrington*
Making Tudor Dolls' Houses	*Derek Rowbottom*
Making Victorian Dolls' House Furniture	*Patricia King*
Miniature Bobbin Lace	*Roz Snowden*
Miniature Embroidery for the Georgian Dolls' House	*Pamela Warner*
Miniature Embroidery for the Victorian Dolls' House	*Pamela Warner*
Miniature Needlepoint Carpets	*Janet Granger*
More Miniature Oriental Rugs & Carpets	*Meik & Ian McNaughton*
The Secrets of the Dolls' House Makers	*Jean Nisbett*

CRAFTS

American Patchwork Designs in Needlepoint	*Melanie Tacon*
A Beginners' Guide to Rubber Stamping	*Brenda Hunt*
Blackwork: A New Approach	*Brenda Day*
Celtic Cross Stitch Designs	*Carol Phillipson*
Celtic Knotwork Designs	*Sheila Sturrock*
Celtic Knotwork Handbook	*Sheila Sturrock*
Celtic Spirals and Other Designs	*Sheila Sturrock*
Collage from Seeds, Leaves and Flowers	*Joan Carver*
Complete Pyrography	*Stephen Poole*
Contemporary Smocking	*Dorothea Hall*
Creating Colour with Dylon	*Dylon International*
Creating Knitwear Designs	*Pat Ashforth & Steve Plummer*
Creative Doughcraft	*Patricia Hughes*
Creative Embroidery Techniques Using Colour Through Gold	
	Daphne J. Ashby & Jackie Woolsey
The Creative Quilter: Techniques and Projects	*Pauline Brown*
Cross Stitch Kitchen Projects	*Janet Granger*
Cross Stitch on Colour	*Sheena Rogers*
Decorative Beaded Purses	*Enid Taylor*
Designing and Making Cards	*Glennis Gilruth*
Embroidery Tips & Hints	*Harold Hayes*

Glass Painting	*Emma Sedman*
How to Arrange Flowers: A Japanese Approach to English Design	
	Taeko Marvelly
An Introduction to Crewel Embroidery	*Mave Glenny*
Making and Using Working Drawings for Realistic Model Animals	
	Basil F. Fordham
Making Character Bears	*Valerie Tyler*
Making Decorative Screens	*Amanda Howes*
Making Greetings Cards for Beginners	*Pat Sutherland*
Making Hand-Sewn Boxes: Techniques and Projects	*Jackie Woolsey*
Making Knitwear Fit	*Pat Ashforth & Steve Plummer*
Natural Ideas for Christmas: Fantastic Decorationsto Make	
	Josie Cameron-Ashcroft & Carol Cox
Needlepoint: A Foundation Course	*Sandra Hardy*
Needlepoint 1/12 Scale: Design Collections for the Dolls' House	
	Felicity Price
Pyrography Designs	*Norma Gregory*
Pyrography Handbook (Practical Crafts)	*Stephen Poole*
Ribbons and Roses	*Lee Lockheed*
Rosewindows for Quilters	*Angela Besley*
Rubber Stamping with Other Crafts	*Lynne Garner*
Sponge Painting	*Ann Rooney*
Tassel Making for Beginners	*Enid Taylor*
Tatting Collage	*Lindsay Rogers*
Temari: A Traditional Japanese Embroidery Technique	*Margaret Ludlow*
Theatre Models in Paper and Card	*Robert Burgess*
Wool Embroidery and Design	*Lee Lockheed*

WOODCARVING

The Art of the Woodcarver	*GMC Publications*
Carving Architectural Detail in Wood: The Classical Tradition	
	Frederick Wilbur
Carving Birds & Beasts	*GMC Publications*
Carving Nature: Wildlife Studies in Wood	*Frank Fox-Wilson*
Carving on Turning	*Chris Pye*
Carving Realistic Birds	*David Tippey*
Decorative Woodcarving	*Jeremy Williams*
Elements of Woodcarving	*Chris Pye*
Essential Tips for Woodcarvers	*GMC Publications*
Essential Woodcarving Techniques	*Dick Onians*
Further Useful Tips for Woodcarvers	*GMC Publications*
Lettercarving in Wood: A Practical Course	*Chris Pye*
Making & Using Working Drawings for Realistic Model Animals	
	Basil Fordham
Power Tools for Woodcarving	*David Tippey*
Practical Tips for Turners & Carvers	*GMC Publications*
Relief Carving in Wood: A Practical Introduction	*Chris Pye*

TOYMAKING

Designing & Making Wooden Toys	*Terry Kelly*	Scrollsaw Toy Projects	*Ivor Carlyle*
Fun to Make Wooden Toys & Games	*Jeff & Jennie Loader*	Scrollsaw Toys for All Ages	*Ivor Carlyle*
Making Wooden Toys & Games	*Jeff & Jennie Loader*	Wooden Toy Projects	*GMC Publications*
Restoring Rocking Horses	*Clive Green & Anthony Dew*		

VIDEOS

Drop-in and Pinstuffed Seats	*David James*	Twists and Advanced Turning	*Dennis White*
Stuffover Upholstery	*David James*	Sharpening the Professional Way	*Jim Kingshott*
Elliptical Turning	*David Springett*	Sharpening Turning & Carving Tools	*Jim Kingshott*
Woodturning Wizardry	*David Springett*	Bowl Turning	*John Jordan*
Turning Between Centres: The Basics	*Dennis White*	Hollow Turning	*John Jordan*
Turning Bowls	*Dennis White*	Woodturning: A Foundation Course	*Keith Rowley*
Boxes, Goblets and Screw Threads	*Dennis White*	Carving a Figure: The Female Form	*Ray Gonzalez*
Novelties and Projects	*Dennis White*	The Router: A Beginner's Guide	*Alan Goodsell*
Classic Profiles	*Dennis White*	The Scroll Saw: A Beginner's Guide	*John Burke*

MAGAZINES

WOODTURNING ◆ WOODCARVING ◆ FURNITURE & CABINETMAKING
THE DOLLS' HOUSE MAGAZINE ◆ THE ROUTER
BUSINESSMATTERS ◆ WATER GARDENING ◆ EXOTIC GARDENING
OUTDOOR PHOTOGRAPHY ◆ WOODWORKING

The above represents a full list of all titles currently published or scheduled to be published.
All are available direct from the Publishers or through bookshops, newsagents and specialist retailers.
To place an order, or to obtain a complete catalogue, contact:

GMC Publications,
Castle Place, 166 High Street, Lewes, East Sussex BN7 1XU, United Kingdom
Tel: 01273 488005 Fax: 01273 478606
E-mail: pubs@thegmcgroup.com

Orders by credit card are accepted

Also by Meik and Ian McNaughton

and available from GMC Publications

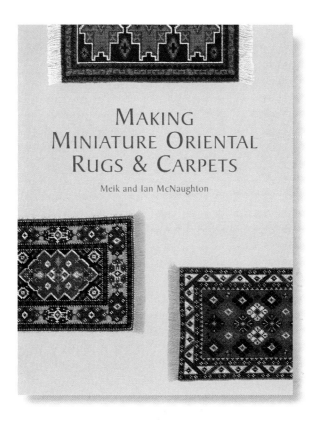

MAKING
MINIATURE ORIENTAL
RUGS & CARPETS

An exquisite collection of twenty-five oriental rug
and carpet designs in 1/12 scale, carefully adapted
from full-size originals and presented in the same
clear format as the present volume

112 pages, 248 x 186mm ◆ Full colour throughout
ISBN 1 86108 066 2